Author: Anne-Marie Saroli
AMGrowthCoaching@gmail.com

Content editor: FriesenPress
Illustrations: via Canva.com
Printer: Rapido livres books

ISBN 978-1-0689169-0-8
Printed in Canada
First Printing
September 2024

Five Stages to practice daily

Dream Big

Pratice Gratitude

See Dream Achieved

Be Patient

Enjoy Success

Dream Big

"Good morning, Jonny . . . Jonny. Hello, Jonny?" Ms. Emery often had a hard time getting Jonny's attention in class.

Jonny was a student at Centennial High who was not only crazy about hockey but who also had a creative imagination. He often daydreamed about being in his happy place, Maple Leaf Gardens in Toronto, playing hockey for the Toronto Maple Leafs. He was obsessed with finding a way to bring his dream to life. And he talked about it ALL the TIME.

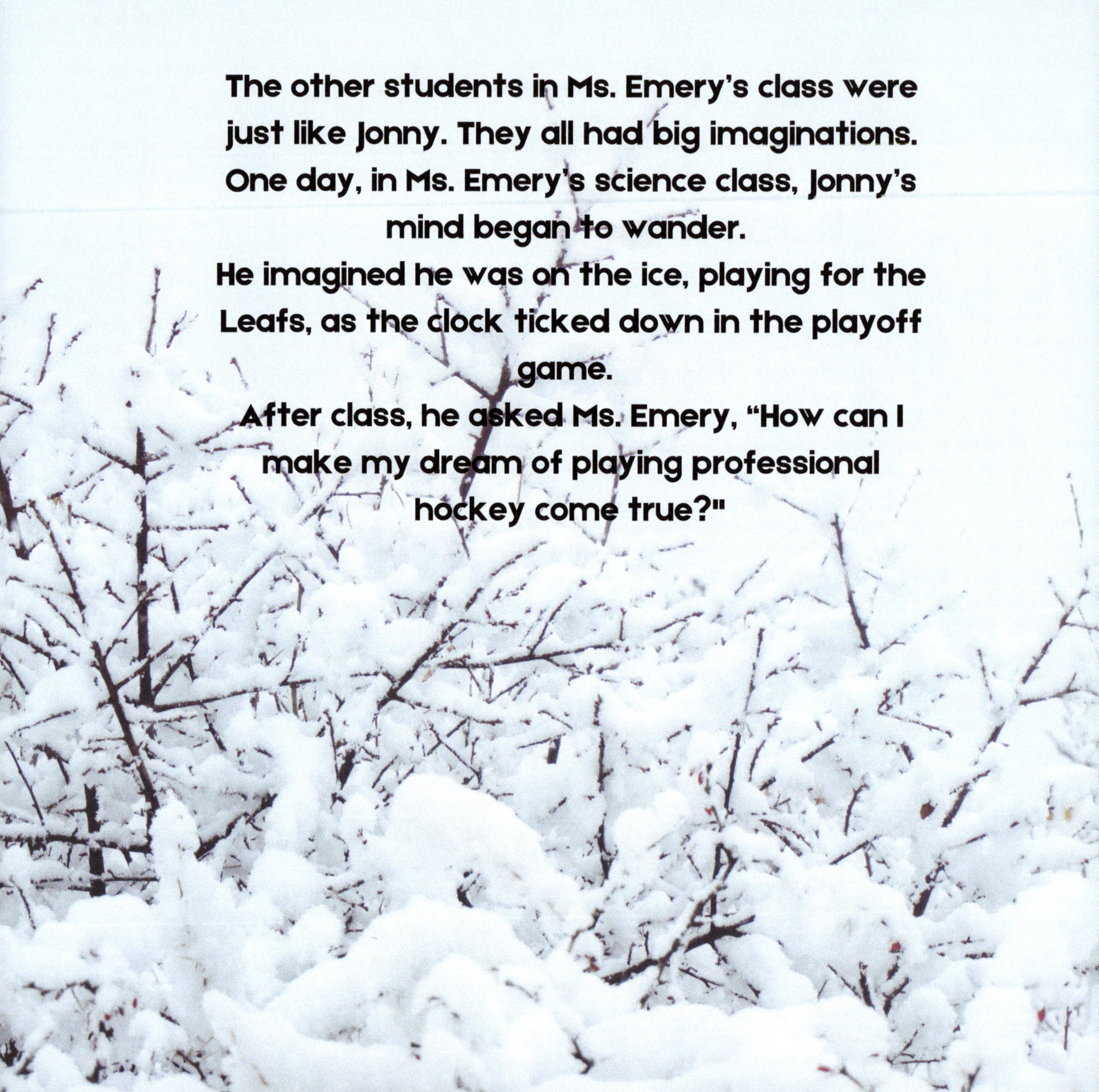

The other students in Ms. Emery's class were just like Jonny. They all had big imaginations. One day, in Ms. Emery's science class, Jonny's mind began to wander.

He imagined he was on the ice, playing for the Leafs, as the clock ticked down in the playoff game.

After class, he asked Ms. Emery, "How can I make my dream of playing professional hockey come true?"

Ms. Emery smiled and replied, "Jonny, it's fantastic that you have such a big dream. Let's talk about this in class."

When you think about your dream, what do you see yourself doing, and how do you feel when you see yourself living in your dream. All of these questions you ask yourself, can help you achieve your dream.

Practice Gratitude

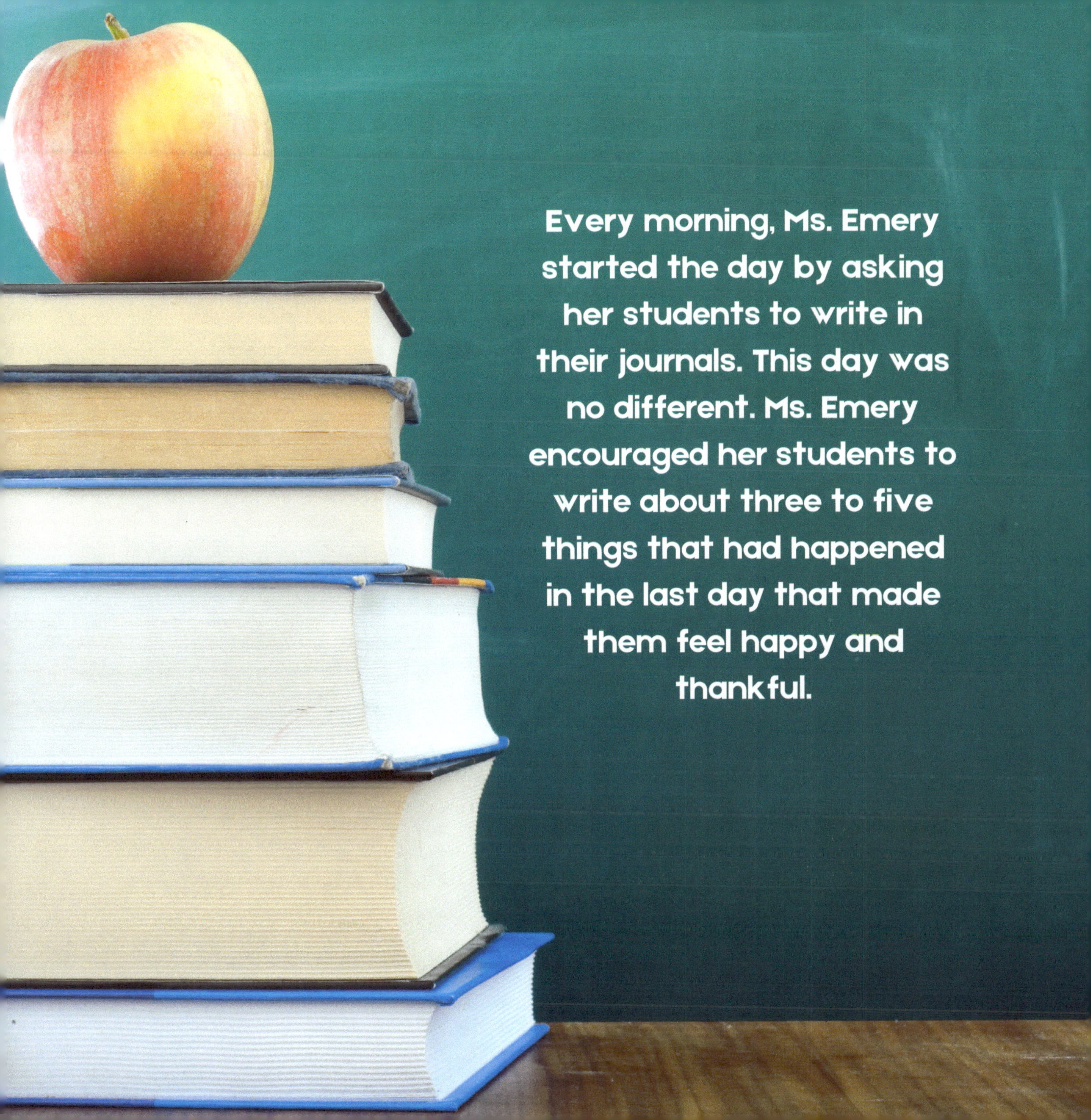

Every morning, Ms. Emery started the day by asking her students to write in their journals. This day was no different. Ms. Emery encouraged her students to write about three to five things that had happened in the last day that made them feel happy and thankful.

"Oh, Ms. Emery, why do we have to write in our journal every day? I write the same things all the time but I don't think it's helping me to get to my happy place or achieve my dream any faster," Jonny shared.

Ms . Emery noticed that many of the students felt the same way. "OK, everyone, let's talk about why it's helpful to write about the things we're grateful for."

"When you wake up in the morning, have you had a restful sleep? Do you have clean and dry clothes to put on? Do you have clean water to wash your face and brush your teeth? Do you have food for breakfast, and a family to share it with?"

She went on, "These may seem like small things. And often, we just expect them to be there for us. But if they weren't there, how do you think you would feel?"

Feeling gratitude, happy, loved for the simple things and for the people in your life, makes us feel happy inside. When we feel happy inside, we are more confident and more resilient, which makes it easier to do hard things, recover from setbacks, and overcome obstacles. Being happy makes us stronger.

Stay Focused

Next, Ms. Emery showed Jonny and his classmates how to concentrate their thoughts and stay focused. She taught them a technique to quiet their wandering minds and focus their energy on being in their happy places and achieving their goals.

notice
your
thoughts

In the morning, when her students were most alert, Ms. Emery encouraged them to sit still for five minutes to quiet their minds. She asked them to sit at their desks with both feet on the ground, and with their elbows and hands lying on top of their desks. Then she set her phone timer for five minutes.

During this time, she asked her students to listen carefully and feel how their chests expanded with each breath they took. Focusing on their breathing allowed their minds to be centered on a specific task for a period of time. Practicing this technique daily helped the students clear their minds, concentrate during the day, and stay calm. It was easy to make it a habit.

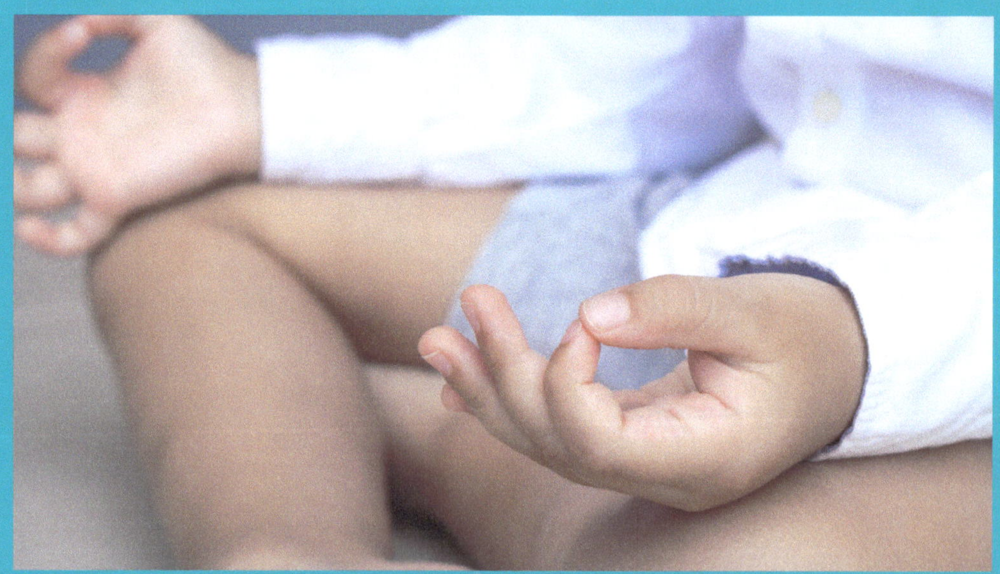

Mindfulness exercises like these, where Jonny learned to clear his mind and focus on the present moment, were really helpful. Ms. Emery explained that by practicing concentration daily, Jonny could build his confidence with little wins, such as achieving a great mark on a test, learning to skate like he was running with ease, or shooting the puck with purpose into the top corner of the net. Jonny's focus helped him feel success, which made his dream feel more real.

Win

Win

See Dream
See Achieved
Achieved

Once Jonny and his classmates understood the importance of daily gratitude and disciplined focus, Ms. Emery encouraged her class to set specific goals to reach their chosen dream. They discussed the steps they needed to take and the actions each of them needed to perform to make their dreams come true.

Ms. Emery had each student write down three to six small steps they had to take to reach their big dream. Jonny wrote down the activities he can work on, learn to skate backwards as fast as he could forward, practice his slap shot to score in the top corners, and make the school hockey team.
Big dreams are achieved by accomplishing a series of small steps.

Next, the students created their own specific vision boards, filled with images related to their dreams. To do this, they cut pictures and phrases they found inspiring out of magazines and newspapers and pasted them all together on a big sheet of paper.

Jonny found a picture of his favourite hockey player and put them in the centre of his vision board.

"YOU MISS 100% OF THE SHOTS YOU DON'T TAKE"

In class, the students talked more about this process. Ms. Emery encouraged them to focus on these images every morning and every night before falling asleep. She said that by visualizing themselves in their happy places, feeling the rush of excitement, and seeing themselves already accomplishing their dreams would help make those dreams come true.

Be Patient

As Jonny learned to write in his journal, focus his thoughts, and visualize success, he also experienced challenges and setbacks. Some days he felt tired or bored, he lost focus and it was hard to imagine his dreams coming true. But Ms. Emery reminded him to do his breathing exercises, stay focused on the present moment, and think about each small step he could take. She told him that perseverance and patience were essential to achieving his goals.

Jonny learned to embrace the ups and downs of his focus, and to see both his successes and failures as learning opportunities. He developed a daily routine to stay committed to his goals and practiced discipline so he could overcome any obstacles that came his way. He found that by being consistent in his thoughts and activities, he could live in his happy place, and keep moving toward his dream.

Enjoy
Success

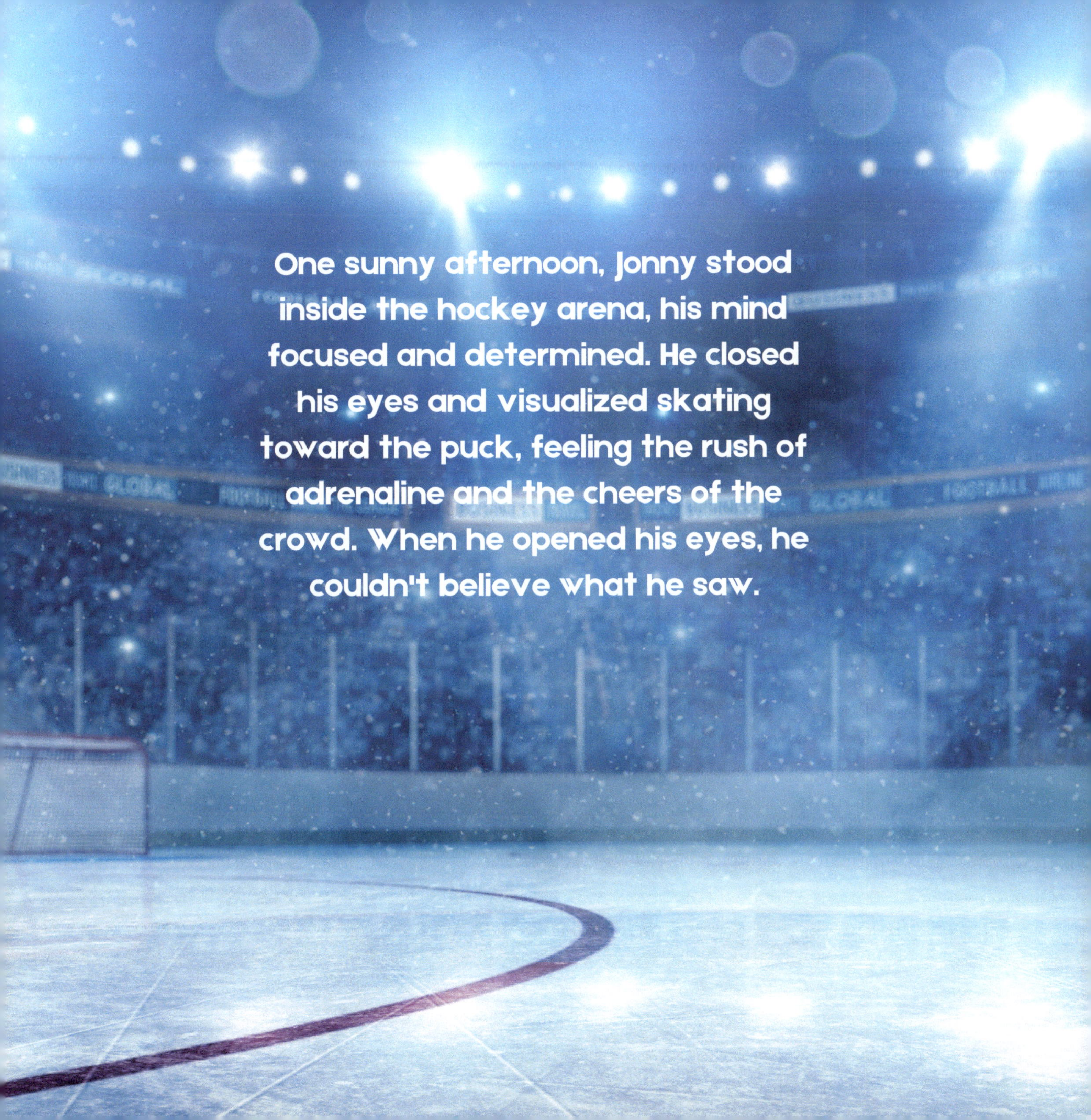

One sunny afternoon, Jonny stood inside the hockey arena, his mind focused and determined. He closed his eyes and visualized skating toward the puck, feeling the rush of adrenaline and the cheers of the crowd. When he opened his eyes, he couldn't believe what he saw.

The arena had transformed into the Maple Leaf Gardens, just like in his dreams. The stands were filled with cheering fans, and the lights lit up the hockey rink. Jonny's teammates, who had also been practicing focus and discipline, joined him on the ice. They played with passion, experiencing the joy and success they had always dreamed of.

From that day forward, Jonny knew that with focus, discipline, and lots of imagination, he could turn his dreams into reality. He continued to work on the power of his mind to excel in hockey and to create a life filled with success. And he shared his newfound knowledge with his friends, family, and teammates, helping them discover their own pathways to success.

Jonny was forever grateful for Ms. Emery and her lessons in gratitude, focus, visualization, and discipline, and for the impact she had made in his life.

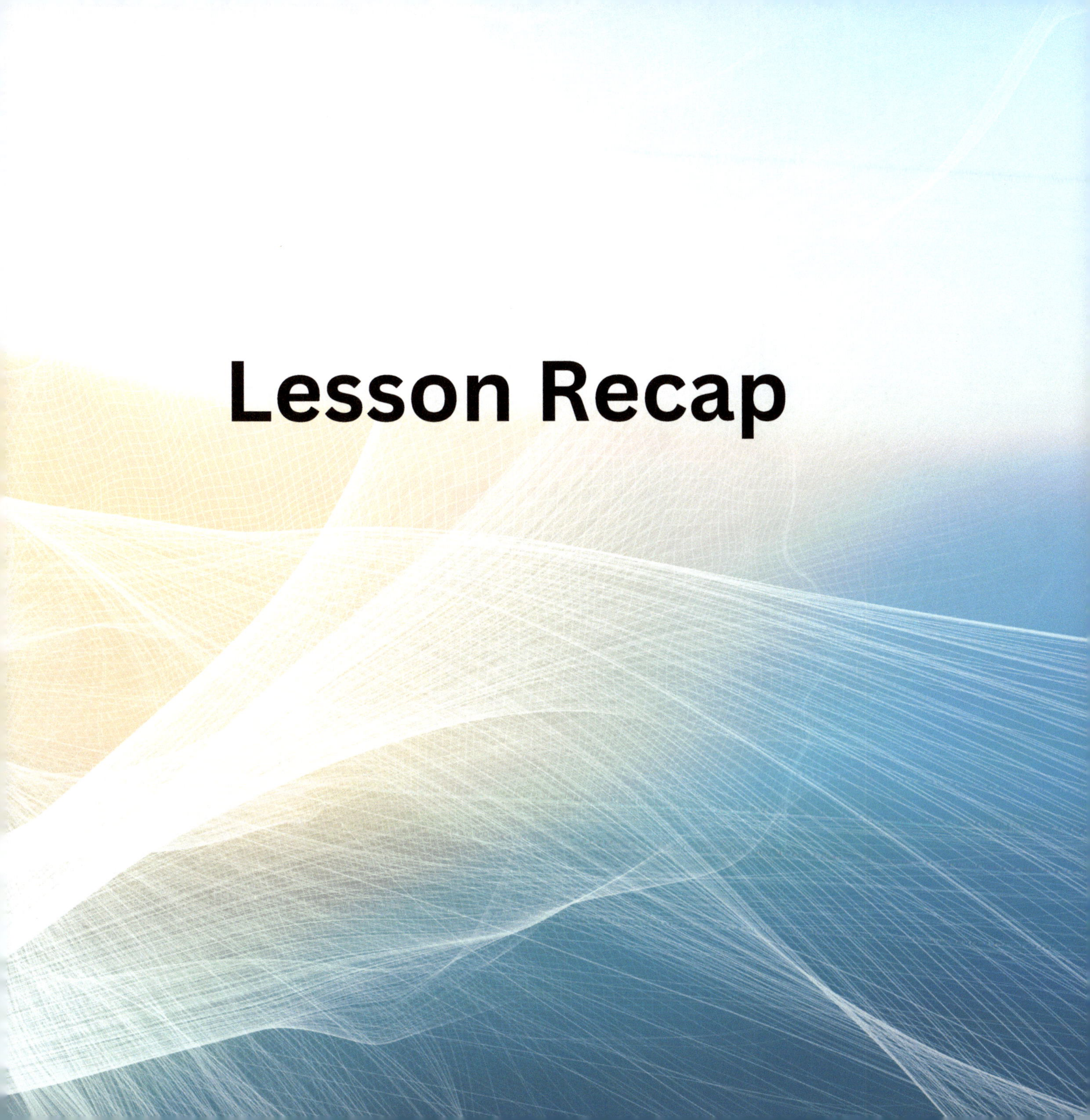

Lesson Recap

Key skills and habits for living from your happy place

Dream Big

Pay attention to how you think about your dream or goal, how often you think about it, how you see yourself currently (self-image), and how you see yourself living in your happy place. And then feel the excitement of living from your happy place.

Practice Gratitude

Create a daily journal where you can write down three to five things that you feel happy about or are grateful for, and concentrate your energy toward seeing yourself living from your happy place.

See Dream Achieved

Keep your goals in mind every day by creating your vision board and updating it with pictures and phrases that inspire you. You are in control of what you focus on. Practice sitting quietly each day, taking deep, calm breaths, to help focus your thoughts and improve your concentration. Remember to pay attention to the small wins you have everyday.

Be Patient

Feel the excitement of achieving your goals, but don't worry if you experience frustration or setbacks. That's normal. Keep focusing your thoughts on your goals, and take it one step at a time. Being consistent everyday is the key.

Enjoy Success

Your current thoughts and focus today will bring you your future success. Small wins lead to the bigger wins.

Believe in yourself, and believe you can accomplish your dreams.
Find your support system to help you achieve a lifetime of living from your happy place.

Glossary

Actions - the process of doing something, typically to achieve an aim

Attitude - a settled way of thinking or feeling about someone or something, typically one that is reflected in a person's behavior

Consistent - acting or behaving in the same way over time

Decision - a conclusion or resolution reached after consideration

Discipline - being able to behave and work in a controlled way which involves obeying rules or standards

Doubt - a feeling of uncertainty or hesitation

Dream - a series of thoughts, images, or emotions occurring during sleep, also, our hopes for our future self.

Feeling - a belief, an emotional state, or reaction

Goal - the end object of a person's effort

Gratitude - feeling thankful for the good things in your life

Habit - any behaviour or action repeated often

Imagination - the power of forming new ideas or images of something not present to the senses

Journaling - the act of keeping a record of your thoughts and feelings

Obsession - an idea or thought that continually takes over or preoccupies a person's mind

Outcome - an end result

Patience - the ability to wait or continue doing something despite difficulties

Purpose - reason for which something exists, is done, or is created

Results - an outcome of something

Routine - a sequence of actions regularly followed

Self-Image - the idea one has of one's abilities, appearance, and personality

Standard - an idea or thing used as a measure for value or quality

Success - the accomplishment of an aim or purpose

Thoughts - an idea or opinion produced by thinking, or occurring suddenly in the mind

Visualizing - to form a picture or mental image of someone or something

www.ingramcontent.com/pod-product-compliance
Lightning Source LLC
LaVergne TN
LVHW071127160826
845679LV00005B/1207

* 9 7 8 1 0 6 8 9 1 6 9 0 8 *